# The Wh the Ladybird Heard Song

Lyrics and melody by Julia Donaldson
Illustrations by Lydia Monks

MACMILLAN CHILDREN'S BOOKS

Once upon a farm lived a ladybird
Who hardly ever spoke a word,
But the ladybird saw and the ladybird heard,
And here's what the animals said:

The cow said, "MOO!" and the hen said, "CLUCK!"
"HISS!" said the goose. "QUACK!" said the duck.
"NEIGH!" said the horse. "OINK!" said the hog.
"BAA!" said the sheep, and "WOOF!" said the dog,
And the old cat miaowed while the young cat purred,
But the ladybird said never a word.

When the little ladybird found out how
Two thieves were planning to steal the cow,
Then everyone kicked up a terrible row,
And here's what the animals said:

"NEIGH!" said the horse.

"OINK!" said the hog.

"BAA!" said the sheep, and "WOOF!" said the dog,

And then both the cats began to miaow,
"We can't let the thieves steal the fine prize cow!"

But the ladybird had a good idea
Which she whispered into every ear.

They waited till night for the thieves to appear,
Then here's what the animals said:

The goose said, "NEIGH!"
and the sheep said, "MIAOW!"
"HISS!" said the horse.
"CLUCK!" said the cow.

"BAA!" said the hen.
"WOOF!" said the hog.
"OINK!" said the cats,
and "QUACK!" said the dog.

Then the duck said, "MOO!", and golly gosh,
The thieves fell into the duck pond —

SPLOSH!

Then the cow said, "MOO!"

and the hen said, "CLUCK!"

"HISS!" said the goose.

"QUACK!" said the duck.

"NEIGH!" said the horse.

"OINK!" said the hog.

"BAA!" said the sheep, and

"WOOF!" said the dog,

And the farmer cheered,
and both cats purred,
But the ladybird
said never a word.

# The What the Ladybird Heard Song
by Julia Donaldson

Once u-pon a farm lived a la-dy-bird who hard-ly e-ver spoke a word, but the

la-dy-bird saw and the la-dy-bird heard, and here's what the a-ni-mals said: The

cow said "Moo!" and the hen said "Cluck!" "Hiss!" said the goose. "Quack" said the duck.

"Neigh!" said the horse. "Oink!" said the hog. "Baa!" said the sheep, and "Woof!" said the dog, and the

old cat miaowed while the young cat purred, but the la-dy-bird said ne-ver a word.
far-mer cheered, _____ and both cats purred, but the la-dy-bird said ne-ver a word.

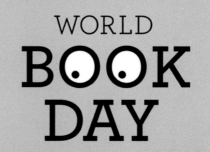

# WORLD BOOK DAY

## 1 MARCH 2012

Want to **WIN** a year's supply of
**BOOKS** for you and your nursery?
*Of course you do …*

This book is by one of our favourite authors (that's why it's in our **HALL OF FAME**!),
but we want to know what *your* favourite book is (or *your* favourite character
– whether it's the baddest baddie or the superest hero)!

It's that easy to win, so visit **WWW.WORLDBOOKDAY.COM** now!

Full terms and conditions apply. See website for details. Closing date: 31 May 2012